Help with Homework

Phonics

Suitable for Grades 1–4

First letter sounds

Write the first letter to complete each word.

_b_all

_nchor

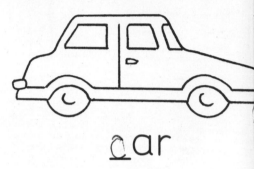

_c_ar

_e_lephant

_d_uck

_f_ish

Hat

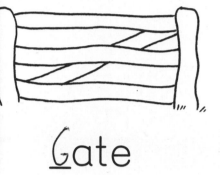

Gate

_gloo

Cangaroo

Jar

Lion

More first letter sounds

Write the first letter to complete each word.

Nurse

Moon

Orange

_uilt

Panda

Rabbit

Table

Sock

Umbrella

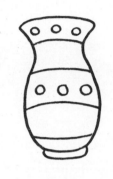

_ase

Watch

X-ray

Yo-yo

Zebra

First letter exercises

Draw a line under the picture that
has the same first sound as the letter at the beginning of the line.
Look carefully, sometimes there's more than one.

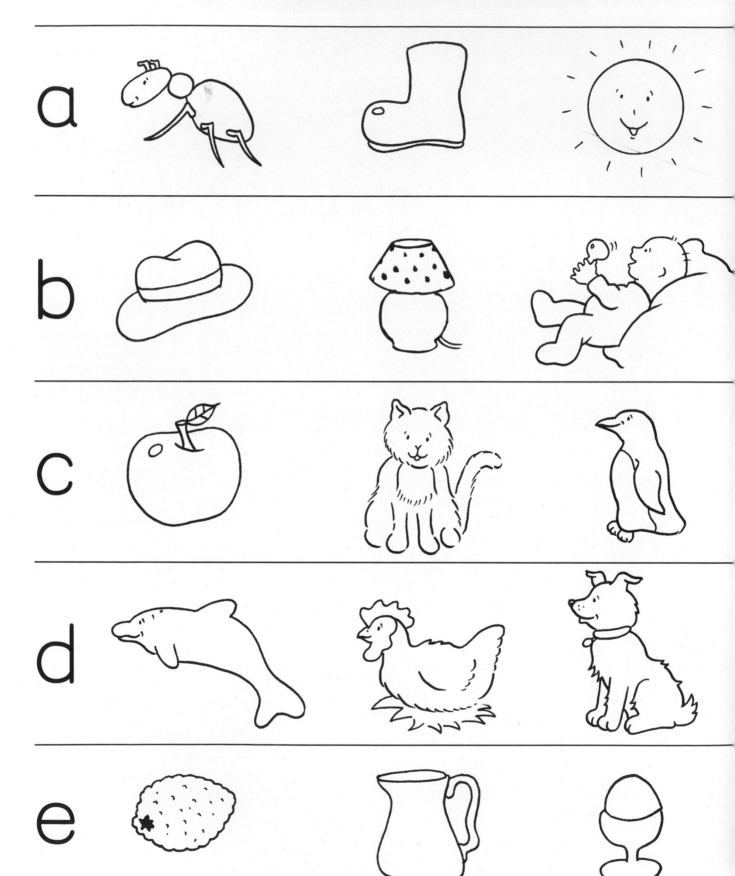

t

u

v

w

x

y

z

Last letter sounds

Write the last letter to complete each word. Use the pictures to help you.

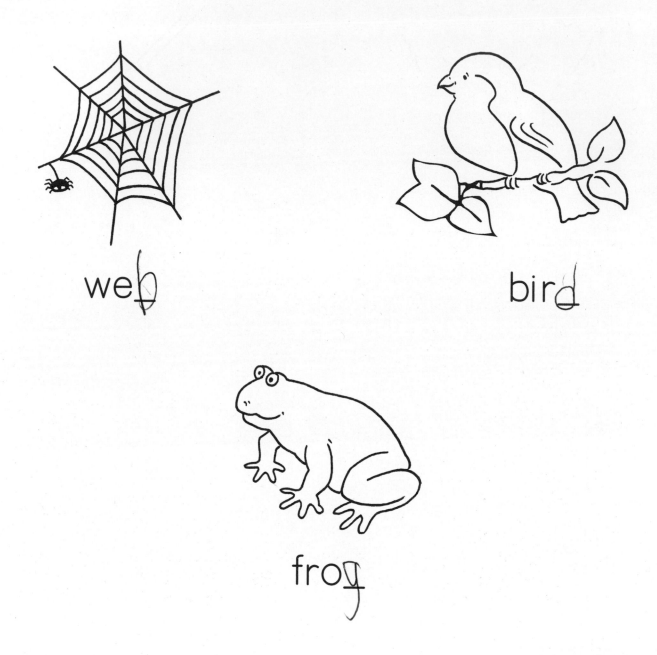

web

bird

frog

ball

jak

hen

mo_

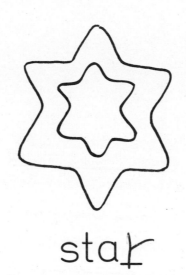

star

cat

fox

Last sounds exercises

Write the last letter to complete each word.

ten

pen

sun

bag

flag

boot

foot

goat

bird

hand

More last sounds exercises

Find the pictures that end with the letter in each box.
Color them red.

First and last letter sounds

The first and last letters are missing.
Write the letters to complete the words. Use the pictures to help you.

Moon

bird

low

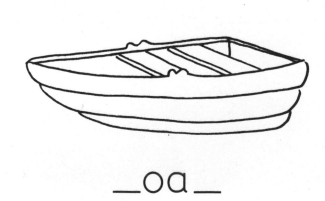

_oa_

_o_

_oo_

_u_

_uc_

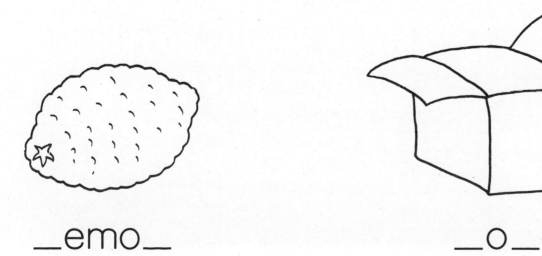

emo

_o_

Middle letter sounds

The middle letters are missing from these words. Write the missing letters to complete the words. The missing letters are all vowels: **a**, **e**, **i**, **o**, and **u**. Use the pictures to help you.

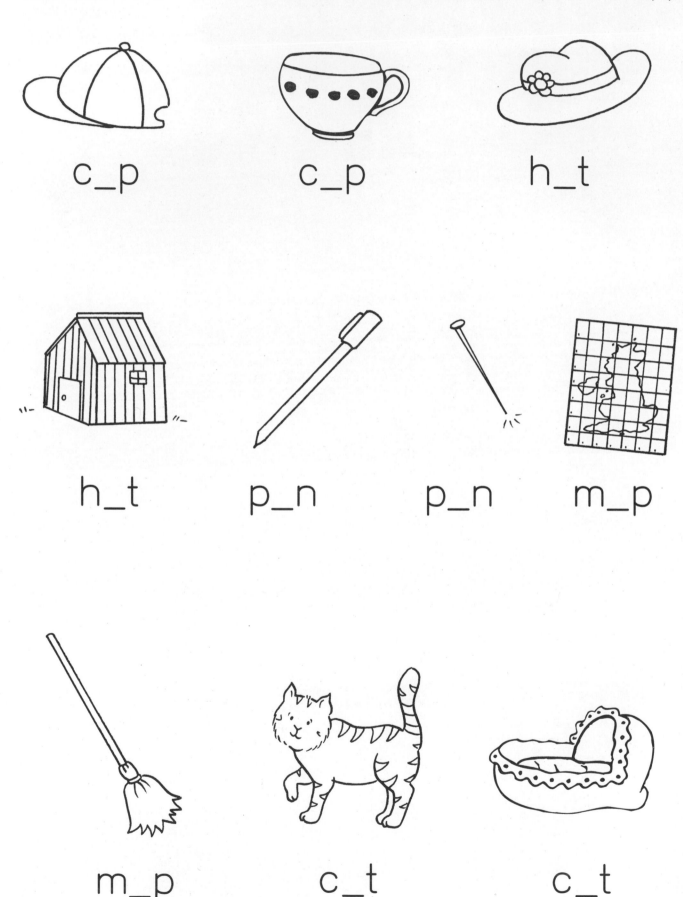

c_p

c_p

h_t

h_t

p_n

p_n

m_p

m_p

c_t

c_t

Middle letter sounds exercises

Write the missing letters.
Draw a line to connect the two pairs that rhyme.

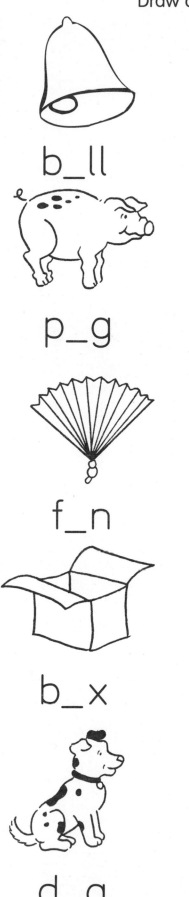

b_ll

p_g

f_n

b_x

d_g

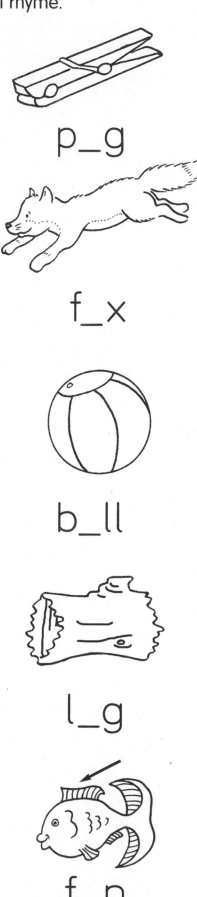

p_g

f_x

b_ll

l_g

f_n

Rhyming words

Look at the pictures in each group of rhyming words and write the first letter to complet
the words. The letters you will write are called consonants.

_at   _at   _at

_en   _en   _en

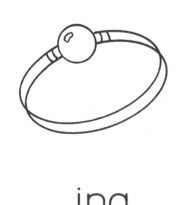

_ing   _ing   _ing

_ock   _lock   _ock

_an   _an   _an

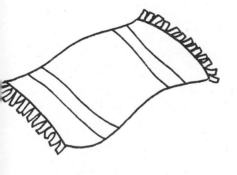

_ug   _ug   _ug

Rhyming words exercises

Look at the pictures in each set.
The words for two pictures rhyme. Draw a line to connect them, and circle the rhyming words in the boxes.

| ball |
| butterfly |
| wall |
| flower |
| chair |

| mat |
| book |
| vase |
| cat |
| apple |

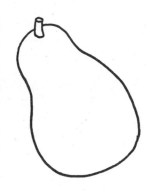

| pear |
| hat |
| fish |
| dish |
| wool |

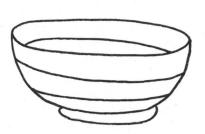

| mitten |
| ladder |
| scissors |
| kitten |
| clock |

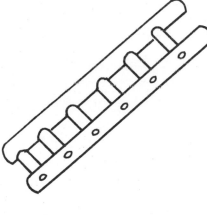

Sound patterns

Sometimes double letters are used to make a longer sound.
These can be vowels or consonants.
Write the missing letters to complete the words.

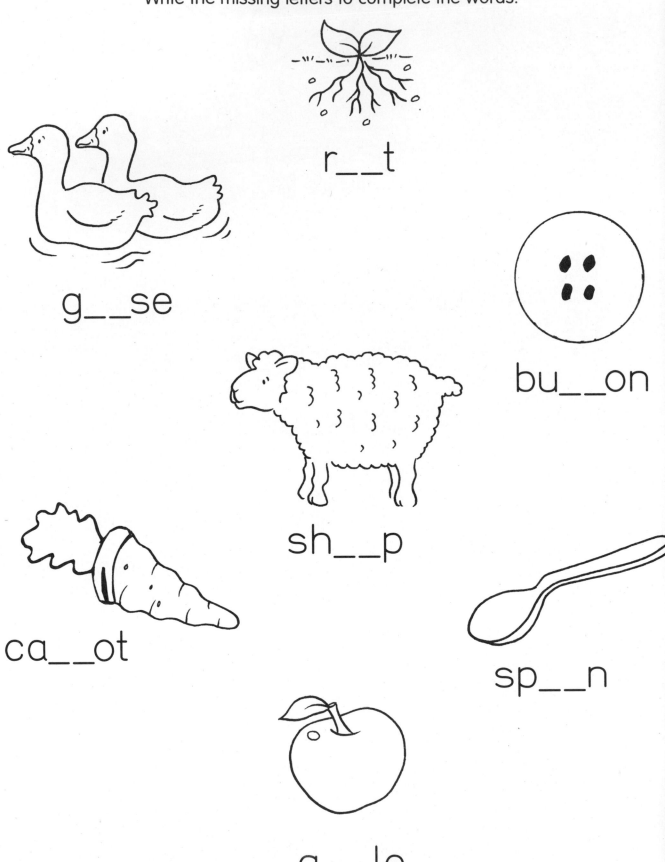

r__t

g__se

bu__on

sh__p

ca__ot

sp__n

a__le

pu__y

pa__ot

b__t

f__t

ball__n

m__n

ki__en

g__se

tr__

More sound patterns

Two different vowels are used together to make a sound.
Sometimes this makes a longer sound, but not always.
Write the missing letters to complete the words.

ea

l__f   p__ch   __gle

ou

h__se   cl__d   f__ntain

ow

cl__n   t__el   sh__er

ai

tr__n   p__nt   sn__l

oa

b__t   g__t   s__p

Double last letters

Some words have double letters at the end to make a longer sound.
Write the missing letters to complete the words.

ba_ _

e_ _

we_ _

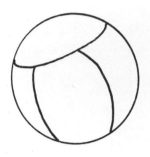

gla_ _

b_ _

z_ _ _

Double last letters exercises

Complete the words in the box.
Write each word on the lines under the correct picture.

_____

_____

_____

_____

_____

_____

she _____

tr _____

dre _____

hi _____

be _____

kangar _____

Silent e

The letter **e** at the end of a word changes the sound of the vowels.
Look at the example, then add an **e** to each word.

Example:

pin

pine

cap

man

cub

Silent e or not?

Add an **e** where you can.
Put a cross through the words where an **e** cannot be added to make a word.

fish

pip

hen

pig

tub

map

tap

Words that sound the same

Some words sound the same but have different spellings.
Look at the words in the boxes and write words that sound the same.
Use the pictures to help you.

Example:

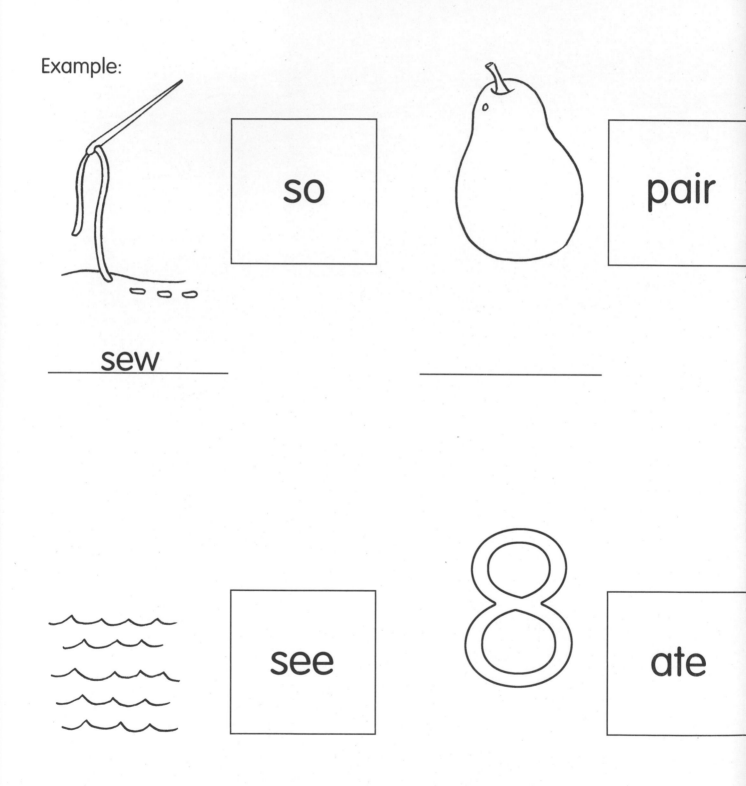

so

pair

___sew___

_____

see

ate

_____

_____

Word search

Look in the grid for words that sound the same as the words above the pictures.
You will find them by reading across or down. Circle the words as you find them.

bear

hare

plane

pear

eight

write

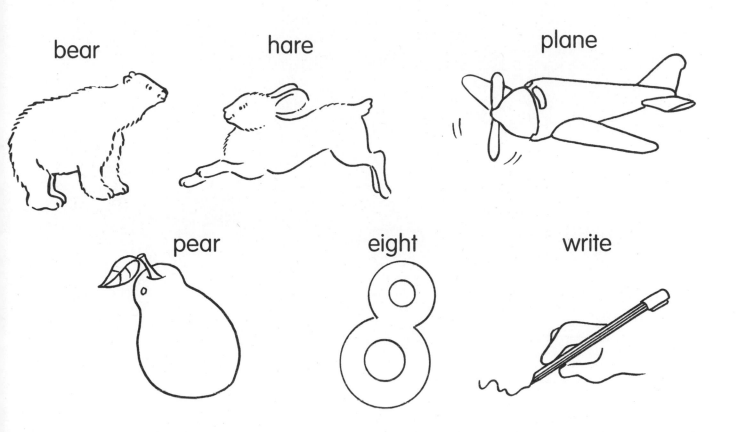

Example:

A	B	A	R	E	H	N	M	K
L	O	T	I	U	Q	T	R	E
A	S	E	C	V	R	G	H	J
N	T	H	D	Q	I	L	I	N
V	C	T	D	T	T	H	N	M
K	P	L	A	I	N	X	C	V
B	H	Y	Q	A	Z	A	I	O
J	A	E	O	O	P	A	I	R
B	I	M	K	L	V	C	D	F
E	R	I	G	H	T	N	M	I

Answers

First letter sounds
anchor ball car
duck elephant fish
gate hat igloo
jar kangaroo lion

More first letter sounds
moon nurse orange
panda quilt rabbit
sock table umbrella
vase watch x-ray yo-yo zebra

First letter exercises

a = ant	n = nose
b = baby	o = octopus
c = cat	p = pan
d = dolphin	q = queen
and dog	r = rake
e = egg	s = snail and sun
f = fork	t = tortoise
g = goat	u = umbrella
h = hat	v = violin
i = ink	w = watch
j = jar	x = xylophone
k = kite	y = yo-yo
l = lamb	z = zebra
m = moon	

Last letter sounds
web bird frog ball jar
hen mop star cat fox

Last sounds exercises
ten pen sun bag flag
boot foot goat bird hand

More last letter sounds
t = boat and hat   m = arm
p = cup   x = box and six

First and last letter sounds
moon bird clown boat fox
cup book duck lemon box

Middle letter sounds
cap cup hat hut pen
pin map mop cat cot

Middle letter sounds exercises
bell ball   pig peg   fan fin
box fox   dog log

Rhyming words
bat hat rat
hen pen ten
ring king wing
rock clock sock
van man fan
rug bug mug

Rhyming words exercises
ball and wall   mat and cat
fish and dish   mitten and kitten

Sound patterns
geese root button sheep
carrot spoon apple
puppy parrot boot
feet balloon moon
kitten tree goose

More sound patterns
leaf peach eagle
house cloud fountain
clown towel shower
train paint snail
boat goat soap

Double last letters
ball egg well
glass bee zoo

Double last letters exercises
shell tree
dress hill
bell kangaroo

Silent e
cap–cape
man–mane
cub–cube

Silent e or not?
pipe tube tape

Words that sound the same
sew–so pear–pair
sea–see eight–ate

Word search

Spelling

Suitable for Grades 1–4

Missing letters

Fill in the missing letters to complete the words.

_nc_or

_o_t

loc

_o_

_le_hant

_r_g

_o_t

_o_se

glo

b_r_

_oa_a

_io_

onke

_e_t

_ran_e

_an_a

_ue_n

_ab_it

_ta_

_i_er

_mbrel_a

_iol_n

_al_us

_ylo_hone

_o-y_

_eb_a

First letters

Complete the words.

_ _ **ead**   _ _ **own**   _ _ **own**   _ _ **ower**

_ _ **ums**   _ _ **arecrow**   _ _ **ide**   _ _ **ail**

_ _ **ider**   _ _ **ool**   _ _ **ing**   _ _ **acto**

_ _ **ig**   _ _ **apes**   _ _ **og**   _ _ **inces**

Last letters

Complete the words.

bas_ _

la_ _

go_ _ _

frie_ _

te_ _

mi_ _

co_ _

wa_ _ _

whi_ _

du_ _

thu_ _

a_ _ _

prese_ _ _

ta_ _

toa_ _ _

pai_ _

Letter ladders

Put a check next to the words that are spelled correctly.

always
allways

before
beafore

children
childran

different
diffrent

earth
erth

knew
knewe

leave
leeve

weight
wieght

beacause
because

opened
openned

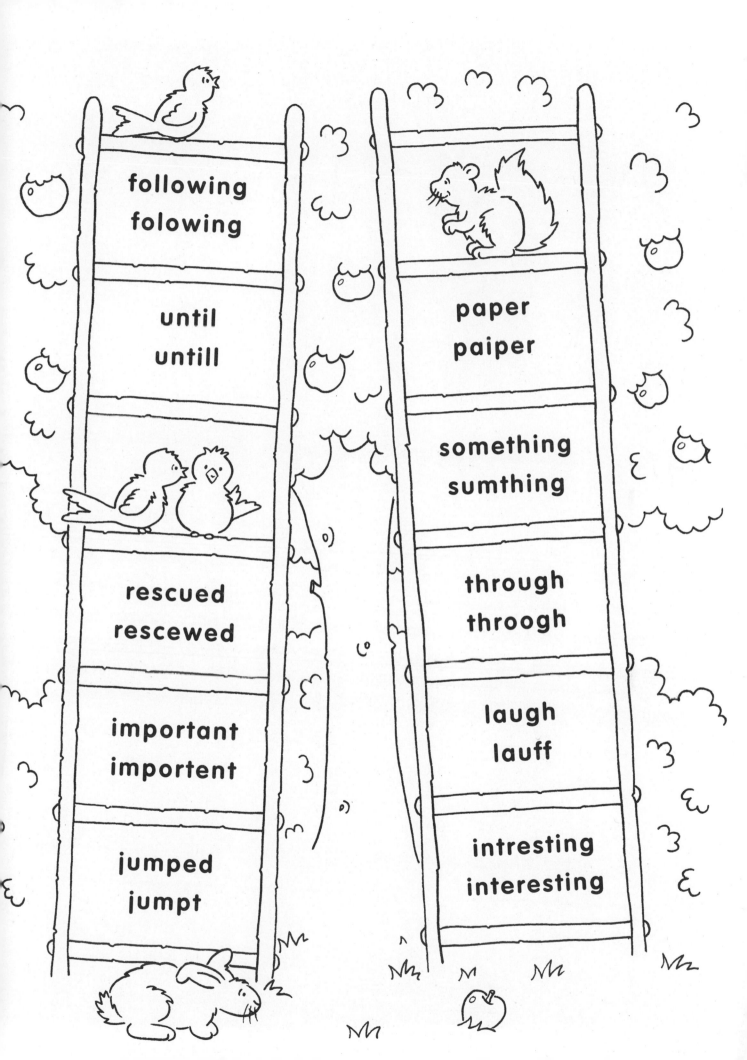

following
folowing

until
untill

rescued
rescewed

important
importent

jumped
jumpt

paper
paiper

something
sumthing

through
throogh

laugh
lauff

intresting
interesting

Days of the week

Fill in the missing letters to spell each day of the week, then complete the sentences.

M_ _ _day

I played s_____ after school.

T_ _ _ _day

I did my h_____ .

_ed_ _ _ _day

I w_____the dog with my grandpa.

_ _ ur _ day

I went s _____ with
my friends.

F _ _ _ ay

I w_____ television
after school.

_ _ _ t _ _ day

I went s_____ for new
c_____ .

S _ _ day

I went on a p_____ with
my f_____ .

What day is it today? Spell it.   _____

What day will it be tomorrow? Spell it.   _____

Months of the year

Fill in the missing letters to spell each month of the year, then complete the sentences.

J_ _ua_y

I make a sn___ m___ .

F_ _r_ _ry

Fl___ ers start
gr___ ing.

_ar_ _

I fl_ my k___ e.

Ap_ _l

L___ bs play in the
f___ ld.

M_ _

Chicks sing in their
n___ t.

_ _n_

I play te___ is.

J_l_

I make cas___ es in the sand.

___g__st

We see some do___ hins.

S___ emb___

The le___ es fall from the tr___ s.

__ t___ er

My umbr___ la keeps me dry.

No__ _m_ er

I eat lots of p_ mpk_ n p___ .

___ e___ er

Santa bri___ s me lots of p___ sents.

Spell the month we are in now. _____

Spell the month of your birthday. _____

Number words

Spell the numbers 1 to 20 on these rocket ships.
Then spell the other numbers in the cloud of smoke.

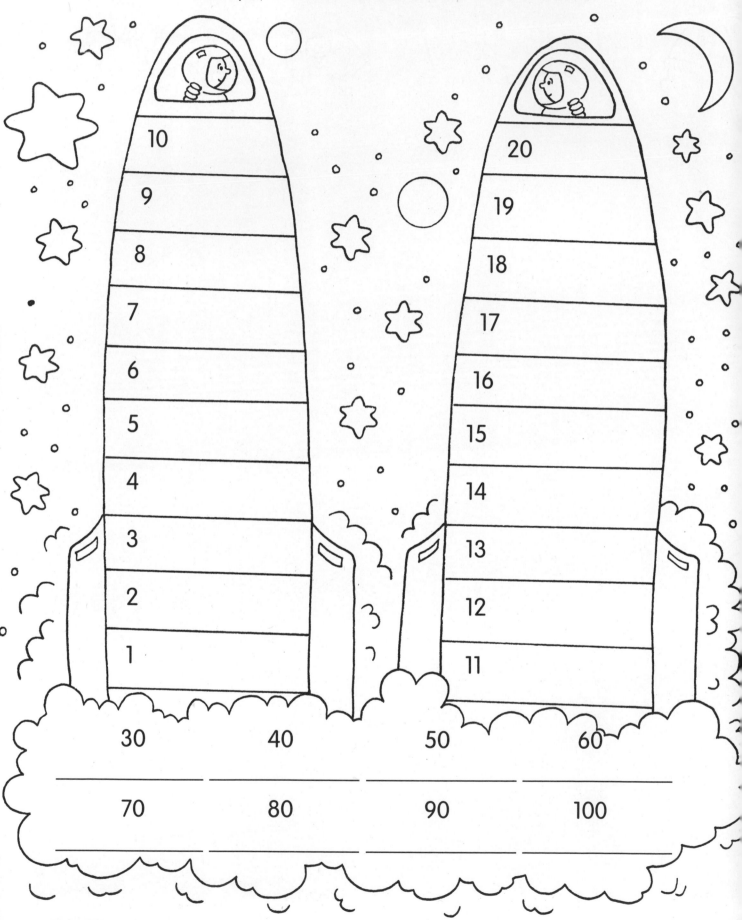

Plural endings

Add the plural endings **"s,"** **"es,"** or **"ies"** to change these spellings.

witch _____

fairy _____

wand _____

cherry _____

toadstool _____

box _____

star _____

book _____

Adding a letter

Add a letter to these words to magically change them into different words.
Write the new words in the boxes.

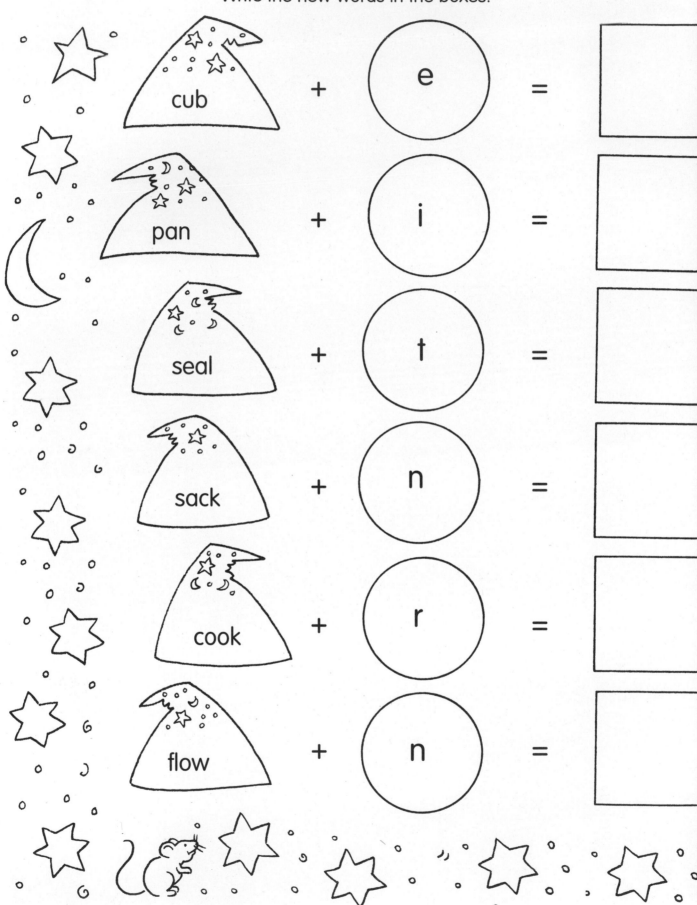

cub   +   e   =

pan   +   i   =

seal   +   t   =

sack   +   n   =

cook   +   r   =

flow   +   n   =

"Magic e" word search

The "magic e" changes the sound of a vowel from a short sound to a long sound.
Look at the pictures and find the words in the grid.
You will find them by reading across and down.
Circle the words as you find them.

```
W E R F G H P N H
C A M L O P I U O
Y K T R E W N A Z
F L P O L E E K A
L I N S O U O M T
B O N E S C A P E
E R F G H B H P A
M J K L O C O N E
Y G A T E W S A G
N D U O M C E W Z
```

Vowel vampire

The vowel vampire has gone batty! Complete the words on the coffins by filling in the missing vowels. The bats are holding the vowels to help you.

h_gh

br__ght

b_f_r_

m_rn_ng

_nd_rst_nd

t_g_th_r

w_nd_w

y__ng

w_th__t

_cr_ss

b_b__s

b_l_w

ch_ng_

m_th_r

g_rd_n_ng

ch_ldr_n

s_st_r

_nd_r

w_rld

_lw_ys

Pumpkin picker

Follow the vowels to help the pumpkin picker through
the field to the tractor.

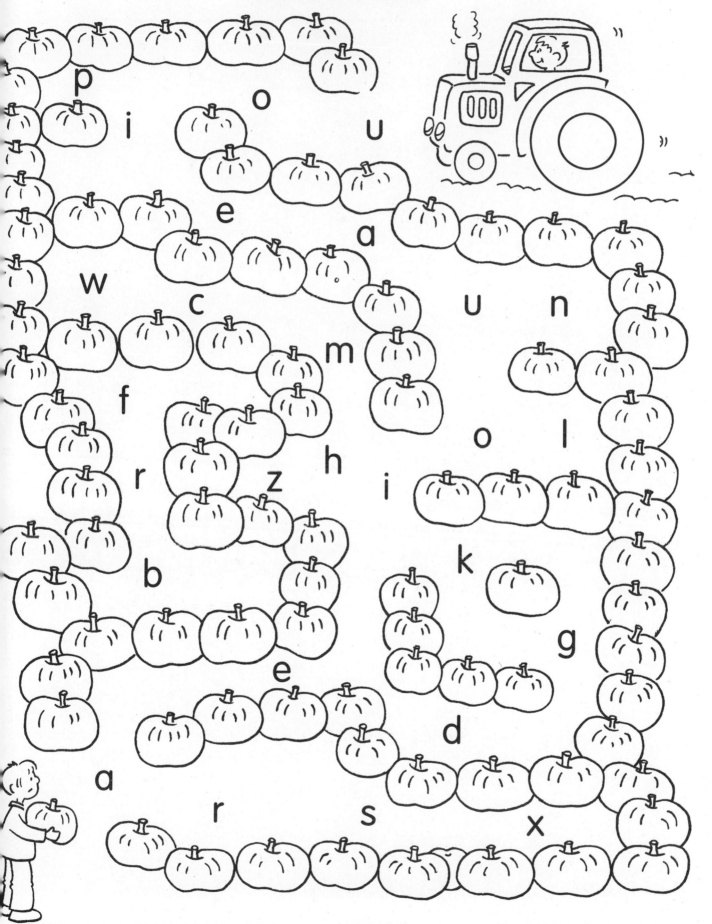

p

i

o

u

e

a

w

c

u

n

m

f

o

l

r

z

h

i

b

k

g

e

d

a

r

s

x

Farm frolics

Complete the words in the speech bubbles by using the following letter sounds:
"ur"   "or"   "er"   "ir."

Rhyme time

Complete these words by adding the missing vowel sounds.
Draw a line to connect the pairs of words that rhyme.

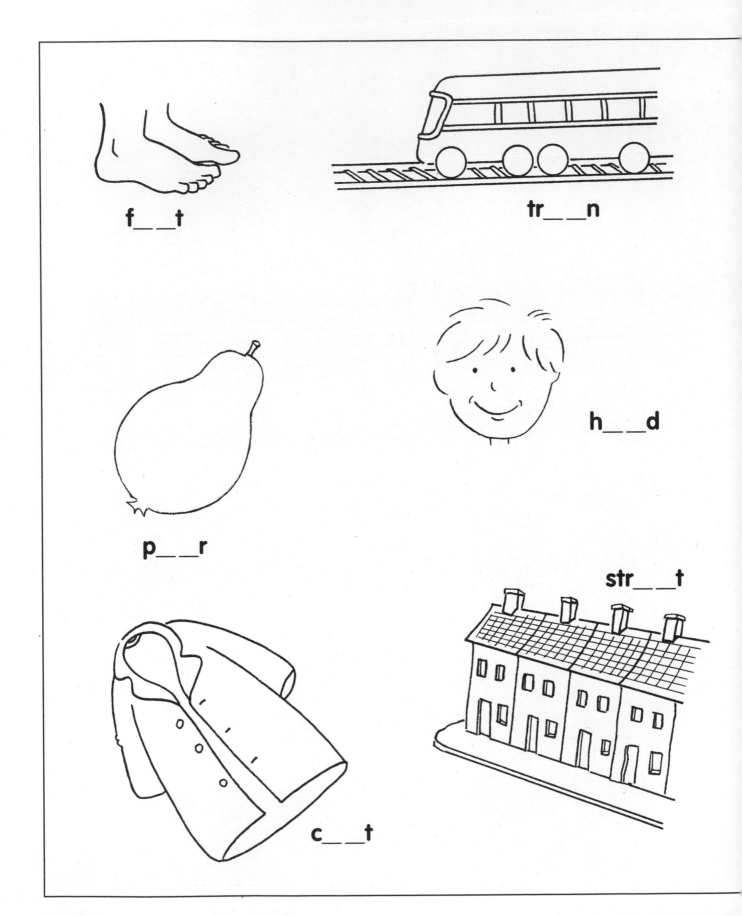

f_ _t

tr_ _ _n

p_ _ _r

h_ _ _d

str_ _ _t

c_ _ _t

br_ _ _d

m_ _ _n

b_ _ _t

b_ _ _r

sp_ _ _n

r_ _ _n

Crossword

The letters **"ou"** and **"ow"** are different letters that can make the same sound.
Follow the numbers across and down, and write the words in the grid.

Wish you were here

The letters **"ai"** and **"ay"** are different letters that can make the same sound.
Complete this postcard by spelling the missing words.

Dear Anna
We are st_ _ing in a little
house by the ocean. On
Tuesd_ _ we went
s_ _ling around the coast.
It started to r_ _n and we
all got very wet! I pl_ _ed
on the beach and found
lots of shells and sea
sn_ _ls. Wish you were here!
Love Gwen

Anna Haynes
101 South Broadway
Missouri
USA
63198

Jungle fever

Unscramble the letters in the vines to spell the names of some jungle creatures.
Write the words. Use the pictures to help you.

Double trouble

Fill in the missing pairs of letters to spell the words
these twins are holding.

sni___   stu___

bu___   we___

ma___   che___

thri___   sma___

bo___   cro___

Space race

Use the letters in the stars to help you spell the words.

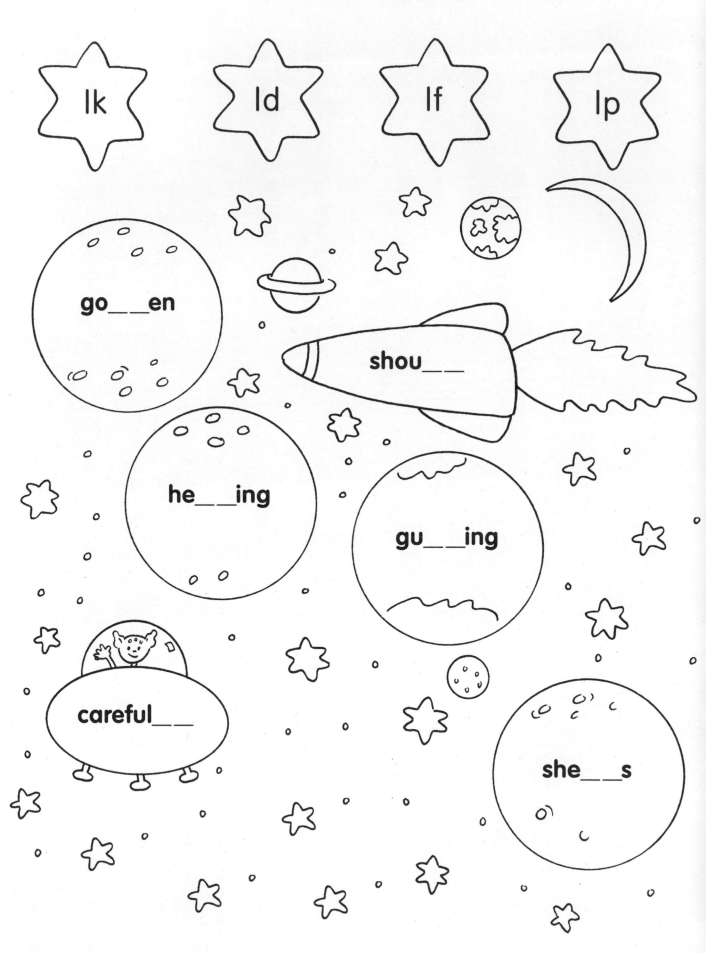

lk

ld

lf

lp

go___en

shou___

he___ing

gu___ing

careful___

she___s

ly   lt   le   ll

mudd___

quick___

cha___

me___

lone___

batt___

midd___

engu___

Snakes and ladders

If you add **"ing"** or **"ed"** to some verbs, you sometimes have to double a letter.
Add **"ing"** or **"ed"** to these verbs. Write the new words in the ladders.
Don't forget—you may have to double a letter!

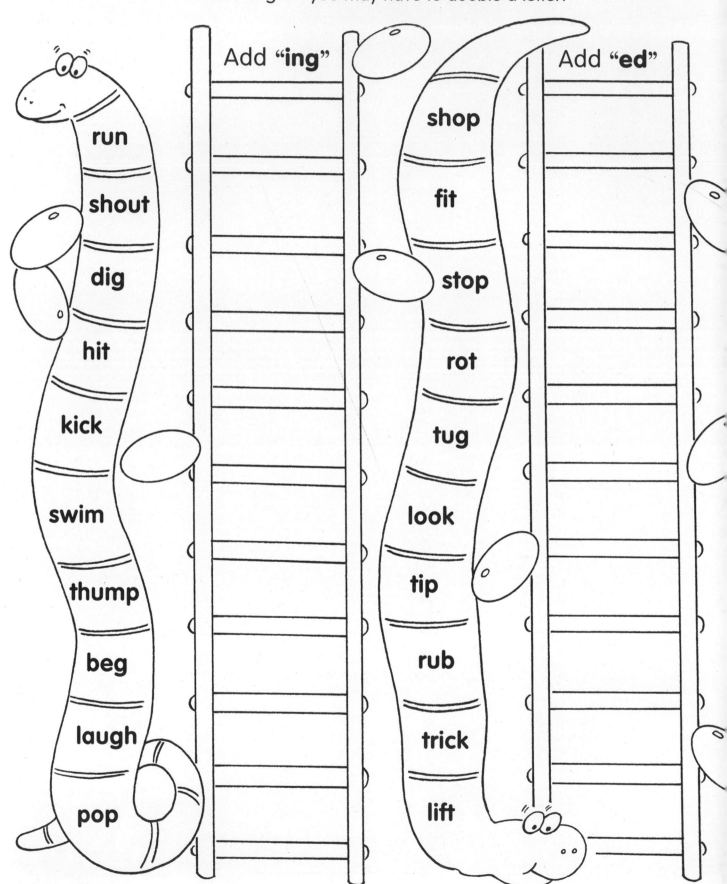

Add **"ing"**

run
shout
dig
hit
kick
swim
thump
beg
laugh
pop

Add **"ed"**

shop
fit
stop
rot
tug
look
tip
rub
trick
lift

"eer," "ere," or "ier"?

Complete these words by adding either "**eer**," "**ere**," or "**ier**."

d_ _ _

t_ _ _

ch_ _ _ _

h_ _ _

st_ _ _ _

volunt_ _ _ _

barr_ _ _ _

car_ _ _ _

Answers

Missing letters
anchor boat clock dog elephant frog goat house
igloo bird koala lion monkey nest orange panda
queen rabbit star tiger umbrella violin walrus
xylophone yo-yo zebra

First letters
bread clown crown flower plums scarecrow slide
snail spider stool swing tractor twig grapes frog
princess

Last letters
basin lamb golf friend tent milk comb wasp whisk
duck thumb ant present tart toast paint

Letter ladders
always before children different earth
knew leave weight because opened
following until rescued important jumped
paper something through laugh interesting

Days of the week
Monday soccer Tuesday homework Wednesday
walked Thursday swimming Friday watched Saturday
shopping clothes Sunday picnic family

Months of the year
January snowman February flowers growing March
fly kite April lambs field May nest June tennis July
castles August dolphins September leaves trees
October umbrella November pumpkin pie
December brings presents

Number words
ten nine eight seven six five four three two one
twenty nineteen eighteen seventeen sixteen fifteen
fourteen thirteen twelve eleven
thirty forty fifty sixty seventy eighty ninety
one hundred

Plural endings
witches fairies wands cherries
toadstools boxes stars books

Adding a letter
cube pain steal snack crook flown

"Magic e" word search

Vowel vampire
high brought before morning understand
together window young without across
babies below change mother gardening
children sister under world always

Farm frolics
word first dirt girl twirl furniture curve modern
burst return
horror interior mayor sword radiator ladder ever
nurse dinner bigger thirsty bird

Rhyme time
feet–street, train–rain, pear–bear,
head–bread, coat–boat, moon–spoon

Crossword

Wish you were here
staying Tuesday sailing rain played snails

Jungle fever
monkeys elephant lizard parrot
tiger snake toucan leopard

Double trouble
sniff stuff bull well mass chess thrill small
boss cross cliff cuff grass glass carrot parrot
pepper popper kitten mitten

Space race
golden should helping gulping carefully shells
muddle quickly chalk melt lonely battle engulf
middle

Snakes and ladders
running shouting digging hitting kicking
swimming thumping begging laughing popping
shopped fitted stopped rotted tugged looked
tipped rubbed tricked lifted

"eer," "ere," or "ier"?
deer tier here cheer steer volunteer
career barrier

Help with Homework

Reading

Suitable for Grades 1–4

Matching letters

Draw lines to connect each penguin to a hat with the same letter.

Draw lines to connect each elf to a fish with the same letter.

Find the letters

Draw circles around the letters you need to spell the word "cow."

Draw circles around the letters you need to spell the word "lion."

Draw circles around the letters you need to spell the word "whale."

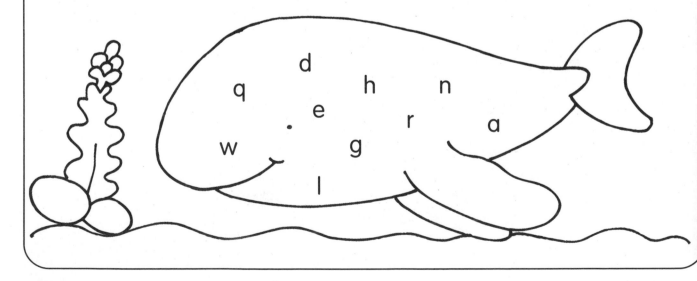

Alphabet blocks

Finish writing the letters of the alphabet on these blocks.

What letters do these toys begin with?
Draw lines to connect each toy with the correct letter block.

Match the words

Draw lines to connect the pairs of butterflies with the same words.

Match the words

Draw lines to connect the monsters with the same words.

Find the animals

Look in the grid for six barnyard animals.
You will find them by reading across or down.
Circle the words as you find them.

M	Y	U	I	P	R	T	E	N
X	K	S	P	S	O	H	J	H
M	S	H	E	E	P	O	V	O
F	O	V	E	Y	I	R	E	R
B	U	E	Q	E	G	T	E	S
H	B	N	E	M	K	Y	O	E
T	I	G	F	Y	A	D	S	X
W	D	O	G	N	E	U	O	J
O	Y	A	U	E	X	C	X	N
M	A	T	L	C	F	K	R	E

Find the footprints

How many times can you find the word "FOOTPRINT"
in this grid? You will find the words by reading
across or down. Circle the words as you find them.

```
I  F  R  F  O  R  T  B  N
X  O  S  P  S  O  H  J  H
F  O  O  T  P  R  I  N  T
A  T  O  Y  I  J  T  F  F
D  P  R  W  E  B  H  T  O
D  R  L  K  L  P  F  O  O
K  I  Y  I  H  U  O  T  T
C  N  E  R  F  P  O  O  P
M  T  Y  U  O  G  T  R  R
C  R  E  S  O  E  P  U  I
Y  K  L  I  T  P  R  I  N
F  O  O  T  P  R  I  N  T
B  K  L  O  R  I  N  H  Y
M  P  L  O  I  H  T  R  D
B  I  T  X  N  E  Y  T  T
K  O  Y  I  T  H  B  M  L
```

Missing vowels

The letters **a**, **e**, **i**, **o**, and **u** are vowels.
Complete these words by filling in the missing vowels.

b_y

g_rl

w_man

b_d

b_th t_b

l_mp

s_n

mo_n

clo_d

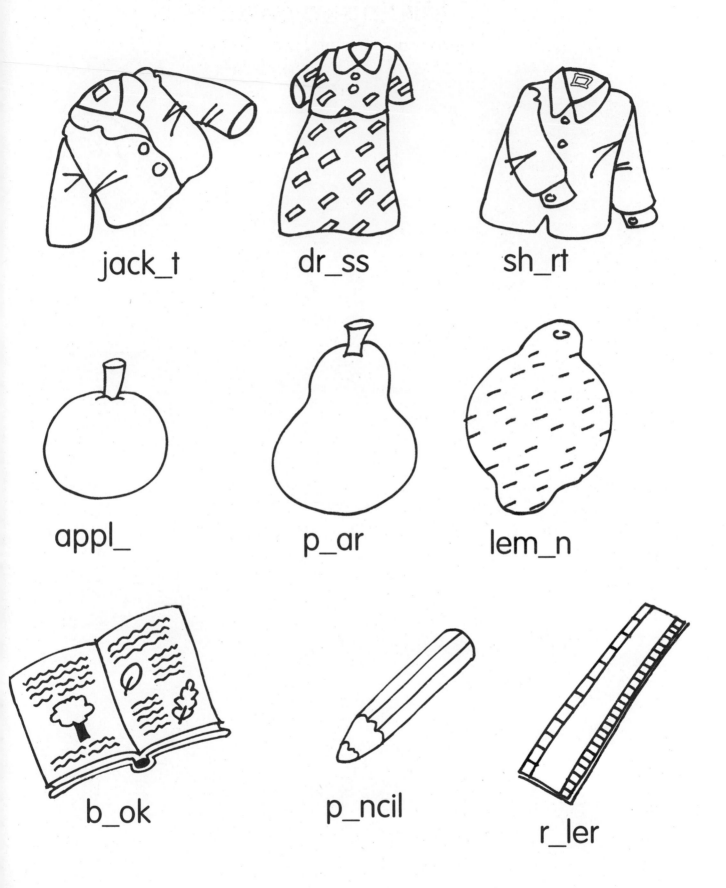

jack_t

dr_ss

sh_rt

appl_

p_ar

lem_n

b_ok

p_ncil

r_ler

Making sentences

Finish these sentences by completing the words. The pictures are clues.

1. The _og chased the ca_.

2. The _ag was full of banana_.

3. The telephon_ is on the t_ble.

4. The rab_it jumped out of the _at.

5. The fro_ swam in the pon_.

6. The mo_ was in the b_cket.

7. The ten_ was held with pe_s.

8. The brus_ was by the ti_.

9. The she_p jumped over the gat_.

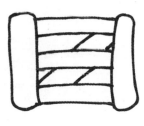

10. The ma_ opened the bo_.

Writing sentences

Finish these sentences by choosing the correct word from the box.
Then write the whole sentence underneath.

| snowman friend kitten kite |

The _____ melted.

John waved to his _____.

The _____ was playing.

Claire loved her new _____.

bee	key	hat	truck

The _____ is on the flower.   She turned the _____.

His _____ was too big.   The man stopped the _____.

Word order

Write the words and punctuation in the correct order to make a sentence.

Fun with words

Make up sentences using each set of words.
You will need to use some other words and punctuation to complete each sentence.

| flowers sun grow |

_____

| bear cave lives |

_____

| boy   window toys |

_____

| spider web made |

_____

Beginning, middle, and end

These sets of pictures make up four different stories.
Put the pictures in order by writing "beginning," "middle," or "end" next to each one.

Gone fishing

Blast off!

Raining again

In the kitchen

Story time

Read the story of Little Red Riding Hood.

Little Red Riding Hood decided to visit her sick grandmother.

When she was picking some flowers in the forest, she met a wolf.

When Little Red Riding Hood arrived at the house, the wolf had dressed up as her grandmother.

"My what big teeth you have," said Little Red Riding Hood.
"All the better to eat you with!" cried the wolf.

The wolf leapt out of bed and jumped on poor Little Red Riding Hood.

Luckily, a woodcutter was passing by and rescued her from the wicked wolf.

Now answer these questions about the story.

1. Who was Little Red Riding Hood going to visit?

_____

2. Who did she meet in the forest?

_____

3. What was she doing when she met the wolf?

_____

4. Who was in grandmother's bed when Little Red Riding Hood arrived?

_____

5. Who saved Little Red Riding Hood?

_____

Rhyme time

Rhyming words sound the same, like "book" and "look."
Connect the words that rhyme by drawing lines between the stars and the planets.

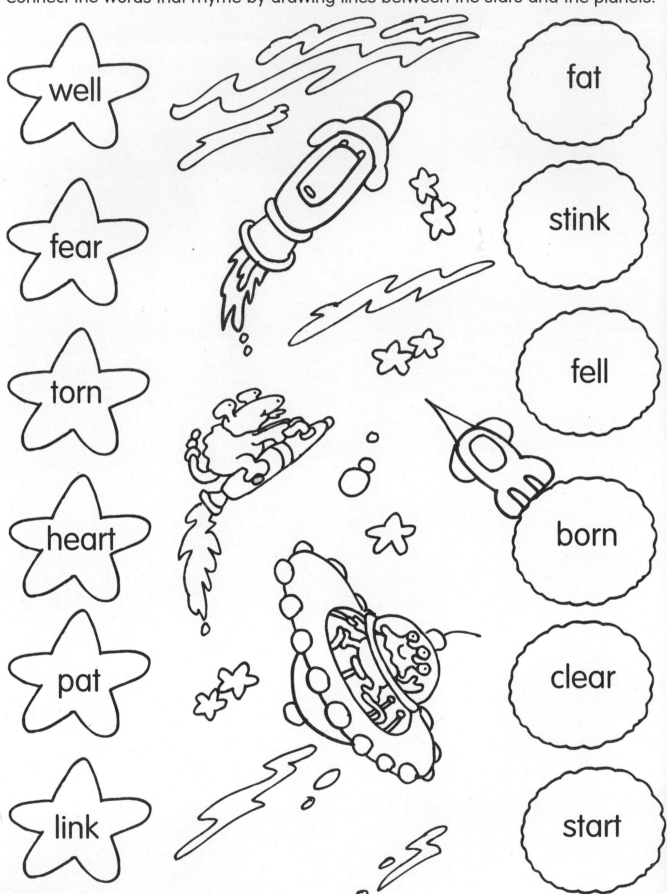

well

fear

torn

heart

pat

link

fat

stink

fell

born

clear

start

Word wall

Look at this word wall. Each row of bricks is made of words that rhyme.

Find the words on the wall that rhyme with the following:

tree	—Color these word bricks red.
mat	—Color these word bricks blue.
tin	—Color these word bricks yellow.
kick	—Color these word bricks pink.
bit	—Color these word bricks green.

pick   lick   sick   tick

pit   fit   sit   hit

bee   tea   me   flea   see

win   bin   sin   fin

bat   hat   fat   sat   pat

Nursery rhymes

Finish these nursery rhymes. Use the words in the boxes.

stile   walked   mouse   crooked

There Was a Crooked Man

There was a crooked man,

And he _____ a crooked mile,

He found a crooked sixpence

Against a crooked _____ ;

He bought a crooked cat,

Which caught a crooked _____ ,

And they all lived together

In a little _____ house.

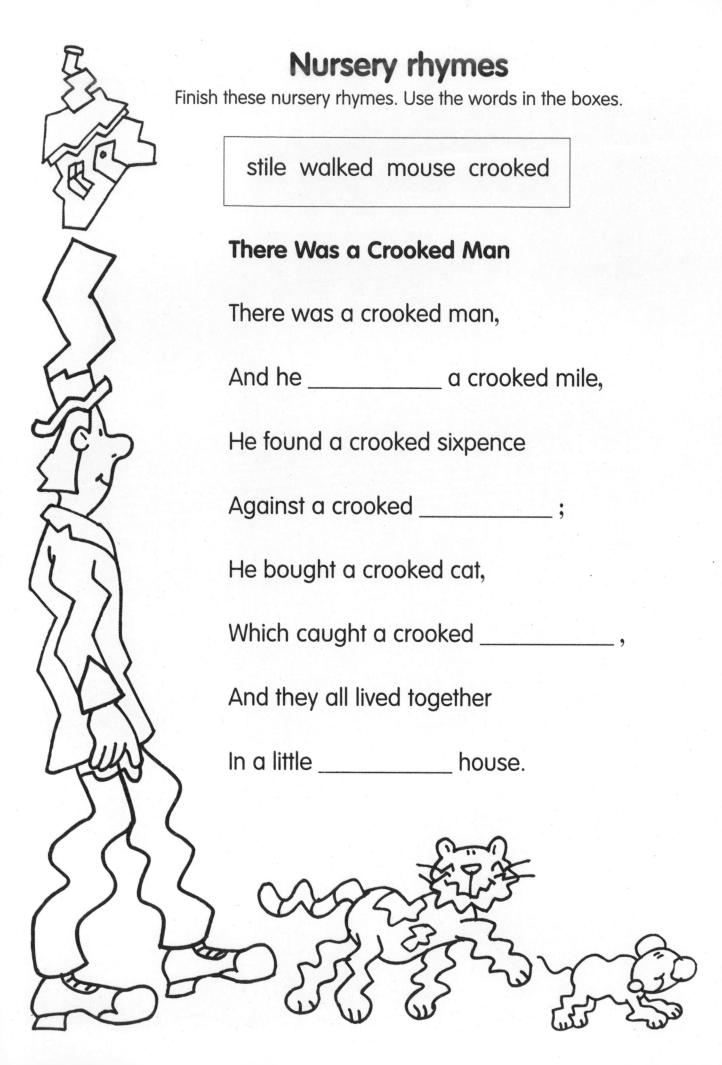

| ten | go | four | finger | you |

One, Two, Three, Four, Five

One, two, three, _____ , five,

Once I caught a fish alive,

Six, seven, eight, nine, _____ ,

Then I let it _____ again.

Why did _____ let it go?

Because it bit my finger so.

Which _____ did it bite?

This little finger on the right.

What's happening?

Write a sentence to go with each picture.

Wish you were here!

Read this postcard from a friend. Write a postcard back to your friend.

Dear Toby,
We are having a great vacation at the beach.
I went fishing and have flown my kite every day. It is very windy here, but the sun has been shining most of the time. How is your vacation? What have you been doing? Hope the weather is good where you are. See you when I get back.
From Kelly

Party time

Read this party invitation from a friend.
Write your reply on the blank card.

Dear Claire

I would like you to come to my birthday party on Saturday July 15 at my house. The party will start at 2 o'clock and end at 7 o'clock. It will be lots of fun. We will play games, dance, and eat lots of yummy food! Please let me know if you can come and what games you would like to play.

From Jane

_____

_____

_____

_____

_____

Circus, circus!

Read this poster about a circus that is coming to town.

The Big Top Circus presents...
Fred the fearless fire-eater,
Justin the juggler,
Clive the crazy clown,
Tracey the trapeze artist,
Alan and his acrobats
... and lots, lots more.
So join us at the Big Top
for a fun-packed evening
to remember!
Date: Saturday July 3
Time: 7pm
Price: adults $2.50
children $1.75
Place: Woodside Park

Check the correct answer to each question about the information on the poster.

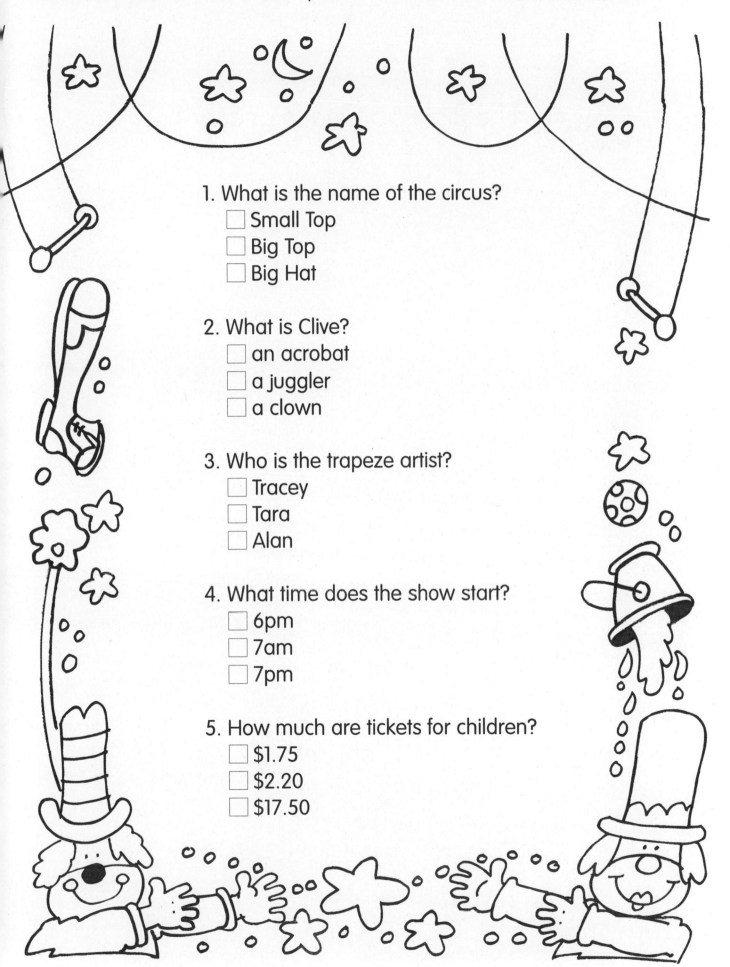

1. What is the name of the circus?
   ☐ Small Top
   ☐ Big Top
   ☐ Big Hat

2. What is Clive?
   ☐ an acrobat
   ☐ a juggler
   ☐ a clown

3. Who is the trapeze artist?
   ☐ Tracey
   ☐ Tara
   ☐ Alan

4. What time does the show start?
   ☐ 6pm
   ☐ 7am
   ☐ 7pm

5. How much are tickets for children?
   ☐ $1.75
   ☐ $2.20
   ☐ $17.50

Answers

Alphabet blocks
b–ball   t–train   d–doll   y–yo-yo   c–car

Find the animals

Find the footprints

Missing vowels

boy girl woman   bed bath tub lamp
sun moon cloud   jacket dress shirt
apple pear lemon   book pencil ruler

Making sentences
1. The dog chased the cat.
2. The bag was full of bananas.
3. The telephone is on the table.
4. The rabbit jumped out of the hat.
5. The frog swam in the pond.
6. The mop was in the bucket.
7. The tent was held with pegs.
8. The brush was by the tin.
9. The sheep jumped over the gate.
10. The man opened the box.

Writing sentences
The snowman melted.
John waved to his friend.
The kitten was playing.
Claire loved her new kite.
The bee is on the flower.
She turned the key.
His hat was too big.
The man stopped the truck.

Word order
I like ice cream.   Where is my hat?
My name is Patrick.   I am six years old.
This is my favorite book. Where do you live?

Fun with words
For example:
Flowers grow in the sun.
The bear lives in a cave.
The boy looked at the toys in the window.
The spider made a web.

Story time
1. She was going to visit her sick grandmother.
2. She met a wolf in the forest.
3. She was picking flowers when she met the wolf.
4. The wolf was in grandmother's bed.
5. A woodcutter saved her.

Rhyme time
well–fell   fear–clear   torn–born
heart–start   pat–fat   link–stink

Word wall
tree–bee see me tea flea
mat–bat hat fat pat sat
tin–fin win bin sin
kick–pick sick lick tick
bit–hit fit sit pit

Nursery rhymes
There was a crooked man,
And he walked a crooked mile,
He found a crooked sixpence
Against a crooked stile;
He bought a crooked cat,
Which caught a crooked mouse,
And they all lived together
In a little crooked house.

One, two, three, four, five,
Once I caught a fish alive,
Six, seven, eight, nine, ten,
Then I let it go again.
Why did you let it go?
Because it bit my finger so.
Which finger did it bite?
This little finger on the right.

Circus, circus!
1. Big Top   2. a clown   3. Tracey
4. 7pm   5. $1.75

Writing

Suitable for Grades 1–4

In town

Fill in the missing letters on these signs.

_AK_RY

GR_C_RY

EAST STR_ _T

_ISH _TORE

REST_UR_NT

A sleepy surprise

This story has gotten mixed up.
Put the story in order by writing the letters in the boxes at the bottom of the page.

A Freddie called his friends over to take a look.

B Suddenly, he noticed a pair of eyes staring at him.

C It was an ordinary morning at the fire station.

D Freddie Fizz was polishing his shiny red fire engine.

E But the fox was frightened and ran back to the fields.

F There, curled up in the corner, was a fox!

1 ☐ **2** ☐ **3** ☐ **4** ☐ **5** ☐ **6** ☐

Good spells!

Wanda Witch has written the ingredients for her favorite spells.
Write them in your neatest handwriting, but be sure to correct her spelling!

whing of bat

skin of snaike

whiska of kitten

shoo of horse

tode slime

snaill shell

wool of lam

green custerd

milk of gote

mane of lyon

tale of rat

egg of oztrich

peacock fether

toenales

webb of spyder

tooth of dragen

Fairy-tale postcards

Use your imagination to finish writing these fairy-tale postcards.
The first one has been done for you.

Dear Snow White,

How are you? The seven of us miss you very much. Grumpy has been really grumpy and Happy has been really sad!
Write back to us soon.

Lots of love,

The Seven Dwarfs

Snow White

The Enchanted Castle

High Mountains

Magical Kingdom

00647

Dear Tom Thumb,

_____

_____

_____

_____

_____

Master Tom Thumb

_____

_____

_____

_____

Hi Grandma,

_____

_____

_____

_____

Love,
Little Red Riding Hood

Grandma

_____

_____

_____

_____

Dear Rapunzel,

_____
_____
_____
_____
_____
_____
_____

Miss Rapunzel

Tall Tower

Dark Forest

Faraway Land

00022

Dear Hansel,

_____
_____
_____
_____
_____
_____

Master Hansel

_____
_____
_____
_____

Dear Rumpelstiltskin,

_____
_____
_____
_____
_____
_____
_____

Rumpelstiltskin

_____
_____
_____

Magic symbols

The Great Alphonso has made the punctuation magically disappear
from these sentences. Rewrite the sentences, punctuating them correctly.
You will need the following:

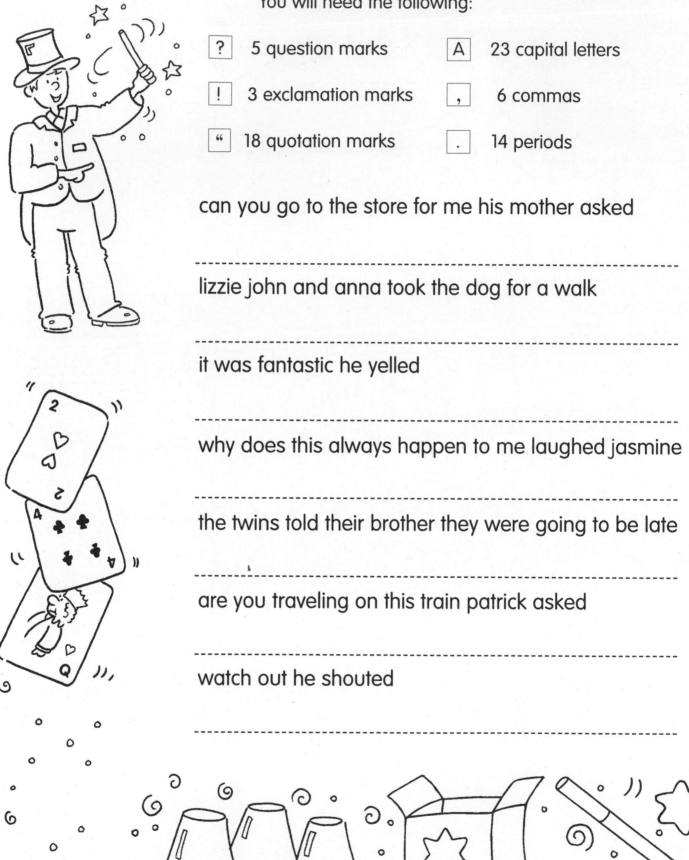

?	5 question marks	A	23 capital letters
!	3 exclamation marks	,	6 commas
"	18 quotation marks	.	14 periods

can you go to the store for me his mother asked

----

lizzie john and anna took the dog for a walk

----

it was fantastic he yelled

----

why does this always happen to me laughed jasmine

----

the twins told their brother they were going to be late

----

are you traveling on this train patrick asked

----

watch out he shouted

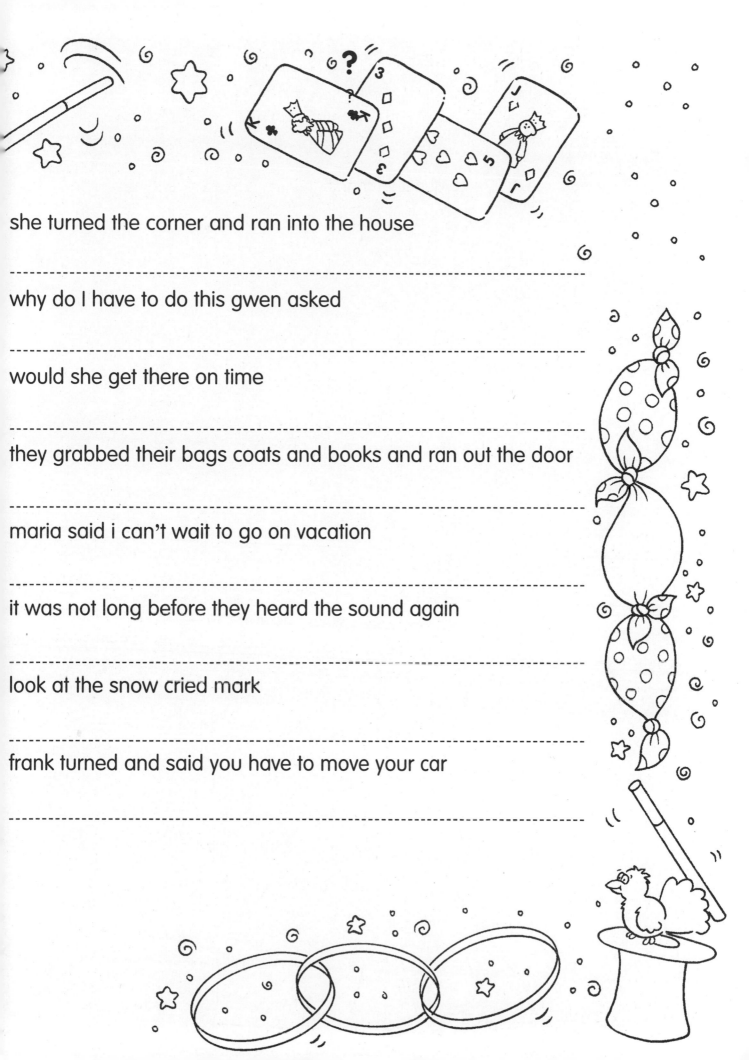

she turned the corner and ran into the house

----

why do I have to do this gwen asked

----

would she get there on time

----

they grabbed their bags coats and books and ran out the door

----

maria said i can't wait to go on vacation

----

it was not long before they heard the sound again

----

look at the snow cried mark

----

frank turned and said you have to move your car

Up, up, and away

Write a story to go with these pictures.
The first one has been done for you.

1. Colin and Claire have always

wanted to take a balloon ride.

2. _____

_____

3. _____

_____

4. _____

_____

5. _____

_____

6. _____

_____

8.

9.

11.

12.

Lights, camera, action!

There are two different storylines hidden in this passage.
Direct the story by circling the words you want to use.
The pictures are clues.

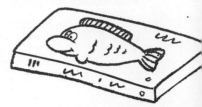

Washington Smith saw the
emerald/fish he had been
searching for, shining in the
eyes/lid of a huge
freezer/statue. He gently
eased himself through the
tunnel/aisle and reached
down into the **freezer/statue**.
With a steady hand, he
carefully lifted the
emerald/fish out and placed
it in his empty
shopping cart/pocket.
He began to hear a
squeaking/rumbling sound.
"Aargh!" he screamed, as a
runaway **boulder/shopping
cart** came hurtling down the
tunnel/aisle toward him.
As he fell to the floor, the
fish/emerald slipped from his
grasp and flew through
the air, falling into the
lair/lap of the angry
clerk/dragon.

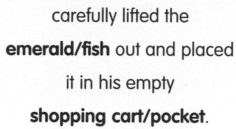

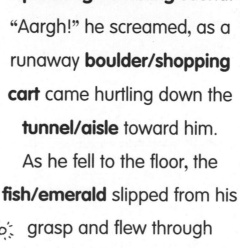

Chewy snack bars

Look at the pictures of these children making snack bars.
Write the instructions to go with them.
The first one has been done for you.

1. Grease a shallow cake pan

with a little butter.

2. _____

_____

3. _____

_____

4. _____

5. _____

_____

6. _____

_____

Vinnie the Vowel Muncher

Vinnie the Vowel Muncher has munched some of the vowels in this paragraph.
Add the missing vowels.

V_nni_ w_s v_ry h_ngry _nd
m_nched s_me _f th_ v_wels
in th_s pi_ce of writ_ng. He
nev_r w_nt to sch_ol _nd d_es
not kn_w h_w m_ny vow_ls
ther_ ar_ in the alphabet.
V_wels jo_n th_ oth_r l_tters
t_geth_r. Th_re ar_ v_ry f_w
w_rds that do n_t h_ve _t
le_st on_ vow_l. Lo_k _t th_
w_y th_ vow_ls beh_ve wh_n
yo_ re_d. The_r so_nds c_n
ch_nge fr_m w_rd t_ w_rd.

How the tortoise got its shell

Read the story and answer the questions below.

The King had invited all the animals to his castle for his wedding feast. Only the tortoise stayed away, and the King did not understand why. So the next day he asked the tortoise why it had not joined the other animals at the feast. "There's no place like home," the tortoise replied. This answer made the King so angry that he insisted that the tortoise carry its house on its back!

Many people would rather live a simple life in the comfort of their own home than live extravagantly in somebody else's.

1. What was the King celebrating?

2. Which animal did not join the celebration?

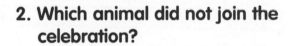

3. What did the King make the tortoise do?

4. Which of the following describes this piece of writing?
a. **a poem**   b. **a fable**   c. **a nursery rhyme**

5. Look at the last sentence in the passage. This is the moral of the story. What is a moral?
a. **a song**   b. **a lesson**   c. **an introduction**

Play poster

Look at the information in the box. Write it in the correct order on the poster.

School Auditorium, Children 75¢, 7:30 p.m., Saturday December 21, Puss in Boots, Adults $1.50, Ivy Bay School presents

The Grand Old Duke of York

Put the rhyme in the correct order by numbering the boxes from 1 to 4.

He marched them up to the
top of the hill,
And he marched them down again.

And when they were up they were up,
And when they were down,
they were down,

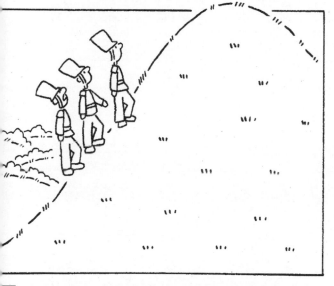

And when they were only halfway up,
They were neither up nor down.

Oh, the grand old Duke of York,
He had ten thousand men;

Down under word search

Look in the grid for six things you might find in Australia.
You will find them by reading across or down.
Circle the words as you find them.

```
K A N G A R O O D U
B O S E V L X N U B
O X M I F Z E E N W
O D E P H K C H O A
M O W O M B A T I L
E L A S I D N Z R L
R O D S O K O A L A
A I T U N Q R C H B
N E E M C F D Q R Y
G A W S U V X N L T
```

Alphabet names

Think of a name for a boy or girl that begins
with each letter of the alphabet.

A _____	N _____
B _____	O _____
C _____	P _____
D _____	Q _____
E _____	R _____
F _____	S _____
G _____	T _____
H _____	U _____
I _____	V _____
J _____	W _____
K _____	X _____
L _____	Y _____
M _____	Z _____

On the shelf

Encyclopedias are information books that are usually arranged in alphabetical order. Look at these encyclopedias and write which book you would look in for the subjects below. The first one has been done for you.

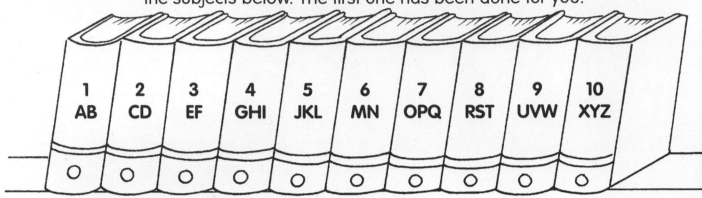

| 1 AB | 2 CD | 3 EF | 4 GHI | 5 JKL | 6 MN | 7 OPQ | 8 RST | 9 UVW | 10 XYZ |

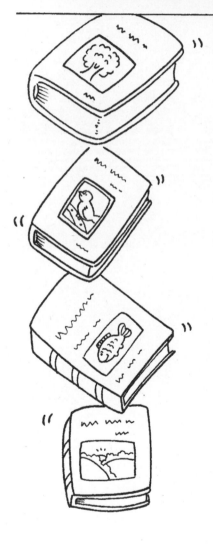

1 antelopes

☐ fishing

☐ juggling

☐ Napoleon

☐ yaks

☐ volcanoes

☐ the Romans

☐ pirates

☐ windmills

☐ dragons

☐ President John Adams

Tense time

The **past** tense tells us what has already happened. The **present** tense tells us about something that is happening. The **future** tense tells us about something that is going to happen. In which tense are these sentences written?

1. **Farmer Green grows potatoes in his fields.**

   _____ past/present/future

2. **Carl the crow ate all the seeds.**

   _____ past/present/future

3. **When we get a scarecrow it will help scare the birds.**

   _____ past/present/future

4. **There are lots of rabbits in the fields.**

   _____ past/present/future

5. **The rabbits dug lots of burrows.**

   _____ past/present/future

6. **The gate to the field is closed.**

   _____ past/present/future

7. **Farmer Green will plant more seeds in the morning.**

   _____ past/present/future

8. **Farmer Green's tractor is red.**

   _____ past/present/future

What's it all about?

Look at the titles of these books. The contents and chapter headings are written next to each one. Look at the questions in the box. Write your answers on the lines.

How Things Work

Contents
Safety First
Wheels at Work
Rocket Power
Electrifying Activity
Glossary and Index

Chapters
Bad News
Abandoned
Discovery at the Field
The Search
Unwilling Hunter
Captured
A Memory

The Midnight Fox

The Complete Book of Gardening

Contents
Designing Your Garden
The Fruit and Vegetable Garden
Decorative Garden Plants
Gardening Techniques
Glossary and Index

A Journey Through Time

Contents
Time Chart
Early Man
The Greeks
The Romans
The Vikings
Index

Mountains and Valleys

Contents
The Changing World
The Restless Earth
Mountain Plants
Mountain Creatures
Valley Dwellers
Glossary and Index

1. Which book is about history? . . . .

2. Which book is about science? . . . .

3. Which book tells you how to grow tomatoes? . . . .

4. Which book is fiction? . . . .

5. All the other books are nonfiction. What do they have in common? . . . . .

. . . .

. . . .

Jock Jackdaw's punctuation

Mischievous Jock Jackdaw has stolen some of the punctuation and capital letters from this story. Can you see what is missing?

The Magic Porridge Pot

Once upon a time there was a little girl who lived with her mother. they were very poor and had nothing to eat One day the girl met an old woman who gave her a little pot. All she had to say was, "cook, little pot, cook, and the pot would cook good, sweet porridge. to make it stop cooking she just had to say "Stop, little pot, stop"

one day when the girl went for a walk, the mother felt hungry and asked the pot to cook But she did not know how to stop it and soon the porridge began to cover the kitchen and then the house it was not long before all the houses in the street were full of porridge

Just as the porridge was reaching the last house in town, the little girl came home and said, Stop, little pot, stop from that day on anyone who wanted to come back to the town had to eat their way through the porridge.

Rewrite the story in your neatest handwriting and add
the punctuation and capital letters.

_____

_____

_____

_____

_____

_____

_____

_____

_____

_____

_____

_____

_____

_____

_____

_____

_____

Barnyard crossword

The pictures are clues to these barnyard things.
Follow the numbers across and down to complete the crossword.

Rhyming balloons

Find the words that rhyme and color the balloons the same color.

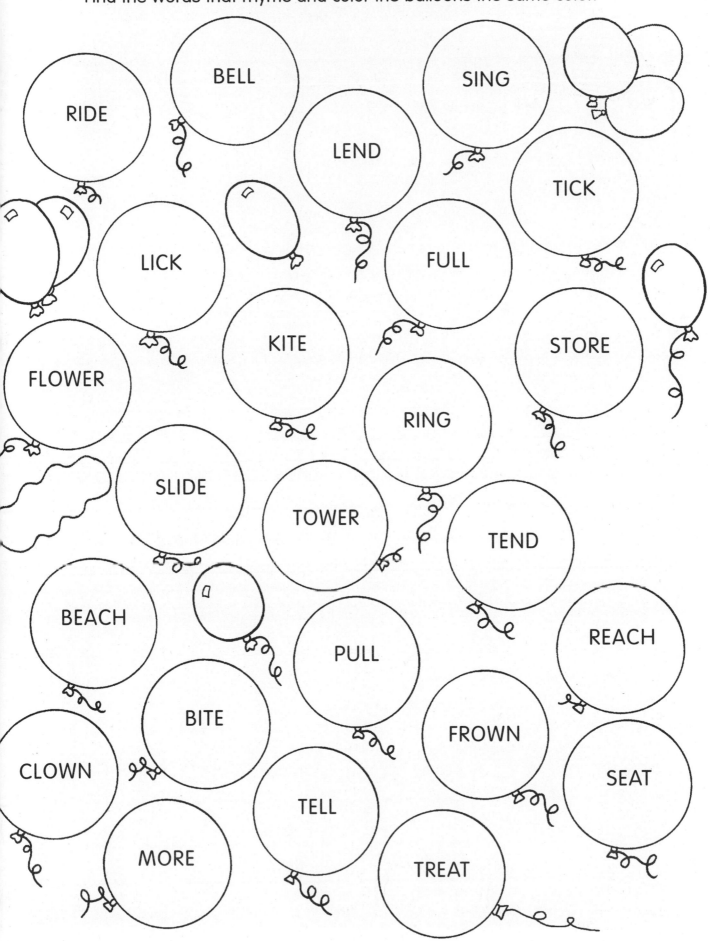

The Three Billy Goats Gruff

Read this story, then answer the questions on the next page.

Once there were three billy goats called Gruff. They lived in the mountains, searching for the fresh, green grass they loved to eat. On the other side of a river was the freshest, greenest grass they had ever seen. The goats trotted toward the river until they came to a bridge.

"The bridge may not be very strong," said the smallest goat. "I will go first to make sure it is safe."

Under the bridge there lived a wicked old troll. When the smallest goat's hooves went trip, trap on the wooden planks, the troll peeked over the edge of the bridge.

"Who's that trip-trapping across my bridge? I'm a troll and I'm going to eat you for my dinner!" he roared.
But the goat replied, "I'm the smallest billy goat Gruff. My brother will be tastier than me." So the troll let the smallest goat go.

Next the middle-sized goat began to cross the bridge. When he was in the middle, the wicked old troll popped up again.

"Who's that trip-trapping across my bridge?" he roared.
"I'll eat you up!"
But the middle-sized goat replied, "Wait for my brother. He is much bigger!" So the greedy troll let the middle-sized goat go.

The biggest goat had seen everything that had happened and smiled to himself. His big hooves went trip, trap on the wooden planks. This time the troll jumped out and stood on the bridge.

"Who's that trip-trapping on my bridge?" he shouted. "Dinner at last!"

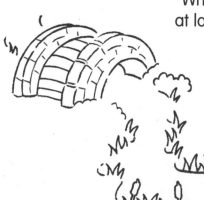

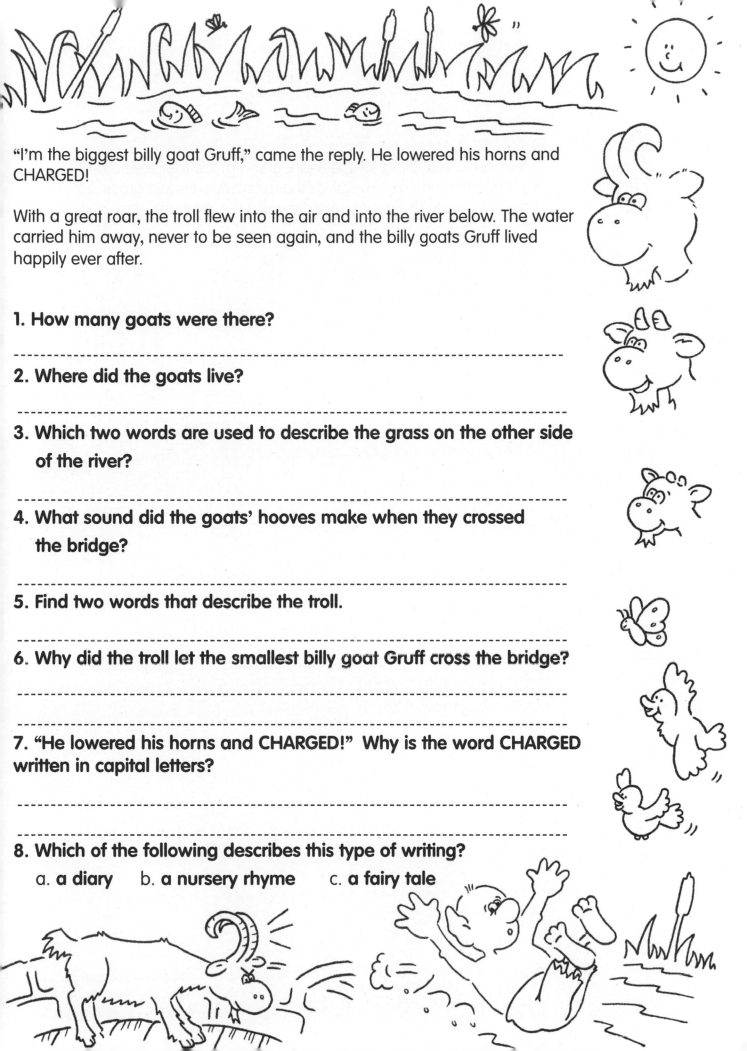

"I'm the biggest billy goat Gruff," came the reply. He lowered his horns and CHARGED!

With a great roar, the troll flew into the air and into the river below. The water carried him away, never to be seen again, and the billy goats Gruff lived happily ever after.

1. How many goats were there?

----

2. Where did the goats live?

----

3. Which two words are used to describe the grass on the other side
   of the river?

----

4. What sound did the goats' hooves make when they crossed
   the bridge?

----

5. Find two words that describe the troll.

----

6. Why did the troll let the smallest billy goat Gruff cross the bridge?

----

7. "He lowered his horns and CHARGED!" Why is the word CHARGED
written in capital letters?

----

8. Which of the following describes this type of writing?
   a. **a diary**   b. **a nursery rhyme**   c. **a fairy tale**

Finish the poem!

Think of the best rhyming words to complete this poem.

I like spring, when the lambs come to play,
During the months of March, April, and _ _ _ .

I think hot summer days are grand!
I go to the beach and dig in the _ _ _ _ .

I like fall, when the winds blow free,
Shaking the leaves from every _ _ _ _ .

I love winter, when there's a snowstorm,
And I'm inside with Pup, all snug and _ _ _ _ .

Answers

In town

MOVIE THEATER STAR WARS BUTCHER CHURCH
PARK DOWNTOWN BAKERY GROCERY
EAST STREET FISH STORE RESTAURANT

A sleepy surprise

1C 2D 3B 4F 5A 6E

Good spells

wing of bat, skin of snake, whisker of kitten,
shoe of horse, toad slime, snail shell, wool of
lamb, green custard, milk of goat, mane of lion,
tail of rat, egg of ostrich, peacock feather,
toenails, web of spider, tooth of dragon

Magic symbols

"Can you go to the store for me?" his mother
asked.
Lizzie, John, and Anna took the dog for a walk.
"It was fantastic!" he yelled.
"Why does this always happen to me?" laughed
Jasmine.
The twins told their brother they were going
to be late.
"Are you traveling on this train?" Patrick asked.
"Watch out!" he shouted.
She turned the corner and ran into the house.
"Why do I have to do this?" Gwen asked.
Would she get there on time?
They grabbed their bags, coats, and books and
ran out the door.
Maria said, "I can't wait to go on vacation."
It was not long before they heard the sound again.
"Look at the snow!" cried Mark.
Frank turned and said, "You have to move
your car."

Vinnie the Vowel Muncher

Vinnie was very hungry and munched some
of the vowels in this piece of writing. He never went
to school and does not know how many vowels
there are in the alphabet. Vowels join the other
letters together. There are very few words that do
not have at least one vowel. Look at the way the
vowels behave when you read. Their sounds can
change from word to word.

How the tortoise got its shell

1. The King was celebrating his wedding.
2. The tortoise did not join the celebration.
3. The King made the tortoise carry its house
   on its back.
4. **b.** a fable
5. **b.** a lesson

The Grand Old Duke of York

1. Oh, the grand old Duke of York,
   He had ten thousand men;
2. He marched them up to the top of the hill,
   And he marched them down again.
3. And when they were up they were up,
   And when they were down, they were down,
4. And when they were only halfway up,
   They were neither up nor down.

Down under word search

On the shelf

3–fishing, 5–juggling, 6–Napoleon
10–yaks, 9–volcanoes, 8–the Romans
7–pirates, 9–windmills, 2–dragons
1–President John Adams ("Adams" not
"President" or "John!")

Tense time

1. present 2. past 3. future 4. present
5. past 6. present 7. future 8. present

What's it all about?

1. A Journey Through Time
2. How Things Work
3. The Complete Book of Gardening
4. The Midnight Fox
5. All of the other books are factual and
   informative. They also have a glossary
   and/or an index.

Jock Jackdaw's punctuation
The Magic Porridge Pot

Once upon a time there was a little girl who lived with her mother. They were very poor and had nothing to eat. One day the girl met an old woman who gave her a little pot. All she had to say was, "Cook, little pot, cook," and the pot would cook good, sweet porridge. To make it stop cooking she just had to say, "Stop, little pot, stop."

One day when the girl went for a walk, the mother felt hungry and asked the pot to cook. But she did not know how to stop it, and soon the porridge began to cover the kitchen and then the house. It was not long before all the houses in the street were full of porridge.

Just as the porridge was reaching the last house in town, the little girl came home and said, "Stop, little pot, stop." From that day on, anyone who wanted to come back to the town had to eat their way through the porridge.

Barnyard crossword

Rhyming balloons

RIDE–SLIDE, BELL–TELL, LEND–TEND, SING–RING, TICK–LICK, FULL–PULL, STORE–MORE, KITE–BITE, FLOWER–TOWER, REACH–BEACH, FROWN–CLOWN, SEAT–TREAT.

The Three Billy Goats Gruff
1. There were three goats.
2. They lived in the mountains.
3. The words "fresh" and "green" are used to describe the grass.
4. The goats' hooves made a "trip-trapping" sound on the bridge.
5. There are three words that are used to describe the troll: "wicked," "old," and "greedy."
6. The troll was greedy and waited for the smallest goat's bigger brother to cross the bridge, because there would be more for him to eat.
7. "CHARGED" is written in capital letters to make the word stand out and to give more emphasis.
8. **c.** a fairy tale

Finish the poem!

I like spring, when the lambs come to play,
During the months of March, April, and **May**.

I think hot summer days are grand!
I go to the beach and dig in the **sand**.

I like fall, when the winds blow free,
Shaking the leaves from every **tree**.

I love winter, when there's a snowstorm,
And I'm inside with Pup, all snug and **warm**.